Memoir Mediocre
MOMENTS MADE MEMORIES

Abdullah Al-Rafi

BookLeaf
Publishing
India | USA | UK

Presentation by *BookLeaf Publishing*

Web: www.bookleafpub.com

E-mail: info@bookleafpub.com

ISBN: 9789358364491

First edition 2022

Dedicated to all those who view my
WhatsApp stories.

Acknowledgement

I would like to acknowledge 4 characters with whom I had the good fortune of developing intimate friendships whilst traversing various stages of my life: Faisal, Murad, Hillman and Muhammad (the last of which who kindly wrote my bio). I would like to thank them for being there for me around the period of my life which yielded the cornerstones for most of the poetry I've written as well as for the joy, support, adventures and perhaps misadventures they provided along the way. These four were my cardinal points, who with all their unique personalities but shared sincerity, helped me navigate through many rough patches. As my friendship with these four will inevitably face its ebbs and flows as life pulls us in different directions, their lasting impressions will always make the partings feel too long and meetings too short.

Thank you guys, I can only hope to return the favour along with my gratitude.

'Tis a Day

Oh what a day.
The wind kisses my cheek;
Cold yet soft.
The sun obscured;
Yet, its light permeates.
It is a day of change;
For good or for worse?
I know not.

Nonetheless it is
A day of change.
But is it the calm
Before the storm,
Or the calm after?
I know not.

One could say,
'Tis a grey day.

Touching Upon Insanity

To touch upon insanity.
To be walking all alone.
Where the line is arbitrary,
Between right and wrong.

The faintest choice available,
To try and maintain control,
Or care not about labels,
And to let the filters fall.

To come upon clarity,
To come upon the why,
Requires a touch of insanity,
Lest the details pass one by.

Then was Now

In the past,
Was once my 'now',
Yet it did not last,
And I discovered how.

How, all my 'thens',
Lead to now,
Which shall again,
To time, bow.

I Wonder...

Upon the shores of sleep I lie,
Reflecting on days gone by,
From the sigh of dawn's call,
Till the deep hue of nightfall.
I wonder...why?

Why did it have to be this way?
Trying to understand what's at play.
Thrust into the depths of my soul,
Wondering where I will find my call.
I wonder...when?

When will it all make sense to me?
The discordant mess become a symphony?
Whatever shall become of me?
Do I fulfil a greater destiny?
I wonder...what?

What must I do to make things clear?
To bravely step off the precipice of fear?
Do I have the courage to pay the price?
To forge a legacy without compromise?
I wonder...who?

Who do I set out to be?
As the tides of sleep bring no clarity.
The waves come to take me away,
To deliver me to another day.
I wonder...where?

Retired

My eyes are tired,
Yet my mind alight,
It's time I retired,
For it's late at night.

However I cannot;
Go into the deep,
Of the blissful realm
Of restful sleep.

Neither hot nor cold,
And I must confess,
Not a worry in the world,
Yet I'm restless.

I try so hard to reach
The dreamy cusp of sleep,
Where our thoughts roam free,
Amongst the memories we keep.

I shall try again,
To escape the awake.
To attain that rest,
I'm so eager to take.

Change

Inevitable.
Eternal.
The universal constant,
Bound to time itself.

Trying to hold on,
To days long gone,
Some becoming tales to be told,
Others lost in memory's fold.

On the infinite edge,
Of yesterday,
Today,
Tomorrow.

Holding tight,
To the cherished past,
As memories take flight,
Little do they last.

Neither rest,
Nor limits.
Always.
Change.

Weary

Going down this rocky road,
How much further will it go?
Tired of this weary load;
The burden forever grows.

Mustering conviction without belief,
That there will be hope to borrow;
That the yesteryears hold relief,
From the darkness of tomorrows.

Lying down in the cold,
Waiting on an epiphany;
To yield or be bold?
On the avenue of destiny.

Hold up against the weight,
Or to let it all come down?
Hold on and believe that fate,
Will bring some ease around?

Sold

The sky is bright,
The air, cold.
The breeze light,
My worries sold.

A brief pause,
To enjoy it all.
The mind claws,
As duty calls.

The cool breeze,
Summer's glow,
The blue seas,
The rivers flow.

Enjoy the hum around,
Or no sound at all,
Let the mind unbound,
Watch the insects crawl.

Moments pass us by,
Wish time would slow,
Give the chance to try,
Appreciate life's show.

Sidelines

What is one to say,
Looking around today.
Where desires are prolific,
The culture, monolithic.

Living on the sidelines,
Like hollow mannequins,
The scent of responsibility,
Have people panicking.

Consumption bordering insanity,
Indulging in unadulterated profanity.
No shape to this society,
An intellectual catastrophe.

No trust, no honesty.
With your soul you pay.
A magnificent travesty,
Of moral display.

All about me,
Myself, and I.
Nothing about we,
Just the modern lie.

ERROR 404

Random Wanderer

I'm just trying to find my way,
Through the darkness of the day,
Through the cold of the night,
Trying to find my light.

I'm just waiting on the rain,
To come wash away the pain,
As I keep trying to borrow,
From the hopes of tomorrow.

Waiting for the sun to rise,
Overcome nightfall's final sighs,
To shine, down on us bright,
Setting a new day alight.

I just try to wander,
The depths of my mind,
As I truly wonder,
As to what I will find.

Time

Tick...Tock.
Tick...Tock.
The water flows,
Yet the rock,
Remains still.
Even then,
It shall change,
As it resigns,
To the touch
Of time.

Falling Fire

I fell for a monster,
Little did I know,
Like a flame,
Bright and beautiful,
Lighting up my soul.
Drawn in like a moth,
I let myself burn.
Yet I regret it not,
For now I know.

Threads

An endless ocean,
Of subjective realities,
Each person a thread,
In the tapestry of humanity.

Weaved across time,
Stories of many lives.
Some most sublime.
Others, dark dives.

Peaks of joy,
Ravines of sorrow,
Procrastination ploys,
Regrets tomorrow.

The ice melts,
The fire burns,
The hurt felt.
Anger churns.

Yet the sun rises,
To bring another day,
With all its surprises,
To wash the pain away.

Rain

Let it rain,
Let it pour,
Let the thunder,
Shake your core.

Embrace the wind,
Feel the cold,
Let the rain in,
Let yourself be bold.

For some semblance of warmth,
For some taste of dryness,
Is it worth resisting,
For an act of self kindness?

Afraid to let go,
Of what comfort holds.
Perhaps let it be so,
Truth be told.

For a While at Least

For a while at least,
I awoke every morning,
Wishing I did not.
For I had in me these beasts.
Fed by dark thoughts.

One day I wrote about rain,
But before it- one of fire,
One of my pains,
And vengeful desire.

Oh the darkness,
Oh the sorrow,
Detesting sleep,
For it'll bring tomorrow.

I let my monsters thrive,
I let them grow,
I let them survive,
Never saying no.

Life took a turn,
As odd as it sounds,
By letting myself burn
Down to the ground.

As I took the dive,
And let them go.
Now I finally feel alive,
Now I know.

Caretaker

As oppression increases,
Our voices have gone cold,
Our hearts of courage famished,
Will we ever again grow so bold?

Where are the bastions of justice?
As we watch chaos unfold.
As we're lambs for the slaughter,
Or do we only have stories of old?

We were supposed to be God's Nation,
As caretakers of this Earth,
Where is justice and peace?
How shall we keep our worth?

Where is our greatness?
In the annals of history alone?
Or is it within each of us,
Just waiting to be shown?

For how long shall we wait,
And let us be preyed upon?
Continue biting the bait,
Of crocodile tear coupons?

We hearken ancient tales,
Of the brave, and the bold.
From Salahuddin to Malcolm X,
There's still a legacy to uphold.

Peripheries

For I, for a long while, had a dream,
Which I determined to be my destiny.
Surely travelling down a stream,
Which broke away unexpectedly.

Now, since foiled were my plans,
Oddly, life takes me places past.
However, this time a different man,
From when I had been there last.

I slowly watch my life reset,
To before this epoch of hurt and joy,
Meeting moments I seldom met,
In this rejuvenating divine ploy.

It has been a leap back to when,
Before I began my failed journey.
So I must start my travel again,
Knowing, I am yet to reach my apogee.

Baffled by my twisted fate,
Erasing recent memories.
Offering a crude blank slate,
To go explore my peripheries.

Shattered

Blurry eyed with tears,
A blessing in disguise,
Blurring together the shards,
Of one's shattered reality,
Making it seem whole again.

Fate Cast

How the good times,
Refuse to last.
The sweet and sublime.
The line of fate cast,
Hooked onto time,
Pulling it so fast,
Leaving nothing,
But the past.

Stillness

There is a sort of stillness I relish,
When the night is cool and calm,
The dark canvas stars embellish,
The moon beckons and charms.

The markers of society still there,
Homes, cars, streetlights and all,
People seeking warmth and care,
Leave the street without a soul.

It is quiet in suburbia,
I shall cherish the silence now,
This momentary utopia,
However long the moment allows.

My Good Face

Showing the world my good face,
As I cloak the evil within,
I ask you Lord by your grace,
To continue forgiving my sins.

Looking to times long gone,
I look until my current day,
I am to my faith a dreaded con,
Oh woe to my misguided ways.

I ask for guidance,
My Merciful Lord,
As our gap widens,
For the sins I scored.

I ask for respite,
My dear Lord,
From Satan's spite,
His snaring cord.

I ask for your love,
My loving Lord,
So I can rise above,
What I can't afford.

My forgiving Lord,
Pardon Your wretched slave, Let Your
words strike a chord,
So I can be of those You save.

Avenues

Wandering through the avenues of time,
Gripping onto what I think is mine.

But as I watch things come and go,
I realise there is nothing that I truly own.

Upon this I surrender to my Lord,
To try reconnect that severed cord.

I know there will be highs and lows,
But also, that the river of mercy flows.

So I repent for the tales of yesterday,
And make sure that is where they stay.

Tomorrow, passing through dawn's door,
I shall enter the day better than before.

I now wander the avenues of time,
Knowing, I shall return to The Sublime.

A While of Healing

It's been a while,
But I haven't let go.
Trying to bring a sincere smile,
But the healing has been slow.

It's been a while since,
I had received that epic blow.
Like a battle worn prince,
The scars will always show.

It's been a while now,
Since I had the fall.
I shall when time allow,
Once again stand tall.

It will be a while till,
I stitch up all the pieces.
Finally discover the will,
To iron out the creases.

There's a while yet,
Till time heals my soul.
To come upon a sunset,
Where I find myself whole.